now you're cookin'
BARBECUE

Colophon

© 2002 Rebo International b.v., Lisse, The Netherlands

This 3rd edition reprinted in 2006.

Original recipes and photographs: © Ceres Verlag, Rudolf-August Oetker KG, Bielefeld, Germany

Design, production, and layout: Minkowsky Graphics, Enkhuizen, The Netherlands

Translation: Vertaalburo Eurolingua, The Netherlands

American adaptation: Josephine Bacon, American Pie, London and Sunnyvale, California

ISBN 13: 978-90-366-1951-6

ISBN 10: 90-366-1951-3

now you're cookin'
BARBECUE

THIS BOOK JUST MAKES YOU WANNA COOK –

REBO
PUBLISHERS

Foreword

This book is for anyone who loves to barbecue. Whatever kind of barbecue you have, you can use it to prepare so many delicious things. And it's fun! Sitting outside with friends or family, chatting and cooking at the same time, that's what barbecuing is all about.

This book will help you make the most of your culinary talents. Delectable recipes include The Perfect T-Bone Steak, Sesame Chicken Wings, Spicy Pork Fillet with Polenta, and Pumpkin with Ginger. Fire up the barbecue, get cooking, and enjoy!

Abbreviations

tbsp = tablespoon

tsp = teaspoon

g = gram

kg = kilogram

fl oz = fluid ounce

lb = pound

oz = ounce

ml = milliliter

l = liter

°C = degree Celsius

°F = degree Fahrenheit

Where three measurements are given, the first is the American measure.

Handy barbecue utensils

Don't forget that barbecues can get very hot—so ensure you have the necessary items at hand before you begin. If you place a small table next to the barbecue, you can arrange the utensils on it that you need, so they are handy.

Requirements for safe barbecuing

Long tongs to move glowing coals or to turn the meat over on a preheated griddle or grill.

Spatulas to turn hamburgers, eggs, and fish or remove them from the barbecue.

Oven gloves to handle hot items.

A long-handled brush to brush the food with oil or marinade.

A fish broiler so you can turn a whole fish safely and easily.

A bucket of water nearby for emergencies.

All sorts of other handy accessories are available, such as aluminum pans and extra grills and griddles which you could buy whenever you feel in the mood.

Before you begin

Cleaning the barbecue

It is very important always to clean the barbecue immediately after use, as food remnants can cause the barbecue to rust. The manual for your barbecue will contain instructions on how best to do this. In general, you can clean the grills and cookie sheets with a stiff brush and cold water, and electric barbecue grills can be cleaned with a plastic dishwashing brush and cold water. Always do this when the barbecue is still slightly warm; as you will clean much faster.

Direct heat method

For this traditional barbecue method, the meat is cooked on a grill or griddle directly over the heat source. This way, the meat is seared and sealed so that the juices cannot escape and the meat takes on a characteristic charbroiled flavor.

If the meat is cooked over a grill, this can cause flames to shoot up when fat drips directly onto the heat source. In this case, place aluminum foil or a griddle under the meat. This method of barbecuing is well suited to thin cuts of that cook quickly.

Barbecuing Methods

Indirect heat method

The heat source is indirect because the heat comes from one side. This way, the meat is cooked more slowly, and is better suited to thicker cuts of meat and whole chickens, for instance. Since there is no flame, this method is also better suited for fattier meats.

advice

There are plenty of excellent barbecue sauces and marinades on the market, you will find them easy to use, and they give fantastic results. If however you want to make your own, here are a couple of interesting ones to try.

Honey & Chili Marinade

Ingredients

¼ cup/60ml/2fl oz red wine

½ cup/120ml/4fl oz honey

¼ tsp/1.25g chili powder

1 tsp/5g mustard powder

Method:

Mix well together

Satay Marinade

Ingredients

½ cup/120g/4 oz peanut butter

½ tsp chili powder

½ tsp ground ginger

2 tbsp lemon juice

1 tbsp brown sugar

½ cup/120ml/4fl oz coconut milk

Method:

Place all ingredients in a saucepan, and stir over low heat until well blended.

Teriyaki Marinade

Ingredients

½ cup/120ml/4fl oz soy sauce

2 tbsp/30g brown sugar

½ tsp/1.25 ground ginger

2 tbsp wine vinegar

1 clove garlic, crushed

2 tbsp tomato paste

Method:

Mix all ingredients together

Herbed Wine Marinade

Ingredients

½ cup/120ml/4fl oz soy sauce

2 tbsp/30g brown sugar

½ tsp/2.5g ground ginger

2 tbsp/30ml wine vinegar

1 clove garlic, crushed

2 tbsp/30ml tomato paste

Method:

Mix all ingredients together

Marinades

Tandoori Paste

Ingredients

2 cloves garlic, peeled

1 in/2.5cm peeled fresh ginger, chopped

1 tsp/5g salt

2 tsp/10g coriander seeds

2 tbsp/30ml lemon juice

2 tbsp/30ml vinegar

1 tsp/5g cumin seeds

½ tsp/2.5g chili powder

1 tsp/5g turmeric

½ cup/120g/4oz plain yogurt

Method:

Blend all ingredients except the yogurt to a smooth paste in an electric blender. Stir into the yogurt.

Soy & Honey Marinade

Ingredients

¼ cup/60ml/2fl oz soy sauce

2 tbsp/30ml honey

1 tbsp/15ml sherry

2 cloves garlic, crushed

1 tsp/5g grated fresh ginger

Red Wine & Garlic Marinade

Ingredients

½ cup/120ml/4fl oz red wine

¼ cup/40g/1½ oz brown sugar

2 cloves garlic, crushed

salt, pepper

Ginger-Rum Marinade

Ingredients

½ cup/120ml/4fl oz unsweetened pineapple juice

⅓ cup/80ml/2½ fl oz light rum

¼ cup/60ml/2 fl oz soy sauce

1 tbsp chopped ginger

2 tsp crushed garlic

1 tbsp brown sugar

¼ tsp chili powder

Lime-Garlic Marinade

Ingredients

1/2 cup/120ml/4fl oz chicken stock

1/3 cup/30ml/2½fl oz lime juice

2 tbsp/30ml olive oil

1 tbsp/15g brown sugar

3 tsp/15g crushed garlic

¼ tsp/1.25g chili powder

¼ tsp/1.25g mint flakes

or ½ tsp/2.5g chopped fresh mint

Moroccan Lamb Marinade

Ingredients

2 tbsp/10g parsley flakes

1 tbsp/15ml lemon juice

¼ tsp/1.25g ground cumin

¼ tsp/1.25g black pepper

¼ tsp/1.25g cayenne pepper

¼ tsp/1.25g ground ginger

¼ tsp/1.25g ground coriander seeds

Method:

Combine all ingredients in a bowl and stir to make a smooth paste. Spread over both sides of lamb and stand for 1 hour at room temperature, or for up to 4 hours in the refrigerator.

Honey, Lemon, and Garlic Marinade

Ingredients

½ cup/120ml/4fl oz olive oil

2 tbsp/30ml lemon juice

1 tbsp/15ml honey

1 tbsp/15g minced garlic

2 bayleaves, crushed

Method:

Mix all ingredients together.

Method

1. Cut the lamb into ½-cm–¼-in cubes. Place into a non-metal bowl and stir in ¾ cup/180 ml/6fl oz of marinade. Cover and marinate for half to one hour or longer in the refrigerator.

Soak the skewers in hot water for 30 minutes.

2. Thread 2 or 3 lamb strips onto each skewer, using a weaving action. Spread them out until they cover two-thirds of the skewer..

3. Heat barbecue until hot. Place a wire cake rack upside down on the grill bars to prevent the marinade burning on the hot grill. Arrange the skewers in rows on the wire rack and cook for 8–10 minutes, turning frequently. Brush remaining marinade from the bowl over the lamb during cooking.

4. Thin down the remaining marinade with extra coconut milk, place in a heatproof bowl, and heat on the barbecue. Remove skewers to a platter and drizzle immediately with the heated marinade.Serve with the dipping sauce.

Ingredients

4lb/2kg boned shoulder of lamb

1 cup/250ml/8oz satay marinade

Dipping Sauce

¼ cup/60ml/2oz satay marinade

Lamb Satay

Method

1. Cut the topside steak into 5 pieces and pound with a meat mallet until thin. Place in a nonmetallic container. Mix the lemon juice, garlic, salt, pepper, and oil together and pour over the steaks. Turn to coat both sides and marinate for 30 minutes at room temperature, or longer in the refrigerator.

2. Soften the butter and spread thinly on both sides of the bread. If desired, mix a little garlic into the butter.

3. Heat the barbecue until hot and brush the grill bars and griddle with oil. Place onions on the griddle. Toss and sprinkle with a little oil as they cook. When they turn transparent, push them to one side and turn occasionally with tongs. Place the bread on the griddle and cook until golden on both sides. Place the steaks on the grill and cook 2 minutes on each side.

4. Assemble the sandwiches as soon as the ingredients are cooked, by placing steak and onions on one slice of toast, topping with a good squirt of steak sauce, and covering with second slice of toast.

Toasted Steak Sandwiches

Ingredients

1lb/500g topside steak

2 tbsp/60ml lemon juice

1 tsp/5g minced garlic

salt and pepper

1 tbsp oil

butter for spreading

10 slices toasted bread

2 large onions, thinly sliced

1 tbsp/15ml oil

steak sauce of your choice

This is a great favorite for backyard barbecue gatherings or fun family

meals. Flat-top barbecues, griddles, or covered barbecues are best, but the

sandwiches may also be cooked on electric barbecue grills, or even under

the broiler. Allow 3 oz/90g lean raw steak per serving.

barbecue

Method

1. Peel the bananas and cut into 1in/2.5cm slices on the diagonal.

Cut bacon into 4in/10cm strips and wrap each strip around a piece of banana.

Secure with a toothpick and brush with honey marinade.

2. Place an upturned wire cake-rack over the grill or griddle of the heated

barbecue. Arrange the bacon-wrapped banana on the rack. Cook 10 minutes,

brushing with marinade, and turning frequently.

Glazed Banana and Bacon Bites

Ingredients

2 or 3 large firm, bananas

4 slices lean bacon

honey & chili marinade (page 8)

Tip

Serve as an appetizer to a barbecue meal or

to accompany barbecue steaks.

Method

1. Trim fat from chops as desired and sprinkle lightly with salt and pepper.

2. Heat barbecue until hot and oil the grill. Place the chops on the grill and sear on one side for one minute. Turn and brush with the Soy & Honey Marinade to glaze. Continue to turn at 2-minute intervals, 4 or 5 times more, or until cooked to the required degree. Take care not to overcook. Cooking will take 10–15 minutes, depending on thickness of chops and type of barbecue used.

3. Place apple rings on the grill about 3 minutes after the chops commence cooking. Turn two or three times, until soft and glazed. Place a sheet of nonstick baking paper under the apples to prevent scorching. If cooking on a charcoal barbecue, use foil that has been brushed with oil.

4. Mix the chili and cooked rice together and heat in a foil or metal dish on the side of the barbecue. Serve the chops with the chili rice and garnish with glazed apple rings.

Ingredients

1cup/250ml/8oz Soy & Honey Marinade (page 9)

6 pork loin chops, ½in/1.5cm thick

salt and pepper

2 large apples, cored and cut into thick rings

2 tsp/10g chili powder

3 cups/660g/22oz cooked rice

Pork Chops with Chili Rice and Glazed Apples

Method

1. Place breast strips in a nonmetallic bowl and stir in around ½ cup/125ml/4fl oz teriyaki marinade. Cover and marinate 30 minutes at room temperature or place in the refrigerator for several hours or overnight.

2. Heat the barbecue until hot. Place a sheet of nonstick baking paper over the grill and make a few slits between the bars for ventilation, or place nonstick baking paper on the griddle. Place the breast strips on the grill and cook 2 minutes on each side, until cooked through and golden. Brush with marinade as they cook. Serve immediately with extra teriyaki marinade as a dipping sauce.

Serving Suggestions:

1. Serve with steamed rice and vegetables.

2. Toss with salad greens to make a hot salad. Dress salad with
1 tbsp teriyaki marinade, 1 tbsp vinegar,
and 3 tbsp salad oil.

3. Stuff into heated pita breads along with
shredded lettuce, cucumber, and onion rings and drizzle
with an extra tablespoon of teriyaki marinade.

Teriyaki Chicken Strips

Serving tips

Serve with steamed rice and green vegetables.
Toss the chicken with shredded cabbage to make a warm
salad. Dress the salad with a mixture of 1 tablespoon
teriyaki marinade, 1 tablespoon wine or balsamic vinegar,
and 3 tablespoons olive oil. Serve with warm pita breads
accompanied by thin slices of pickle and onion rings, and
sprinkle with an extra teaspoon of teriyaki marinade..

Ingredients

1lb/500g chicken breast strips

teriyaki marinade (page 9)

Method

1. Bring the steaks to room temperate. Mix garlic, oil, salt, and pepper together and rub on both sides of the steak. Stand for 10–15 minutes at room temperature.

2. Heat the barbecue until hot and oil the grill bars. Arrange the steaks and sear for one minute each side. Move steaks to cooler part of the barbecue to continue cooking over moderate heat, or reduce the heat, depending on the type of barbecue. If heat cannot be reduced, then elevate the steaks on a wire cake rack placed 1in/2.5cm above the grill bars. Cook until the desired degree of doneness is achieved, 5–6 minutes for rare, 7–10 minutes for medium, and 10–14 minutes for well done. Turn during cooking.

3. Serve on a heated steak plate and top with a scoop of garlic butter.

Serve with jacket potatoes.

Ingredients

4 T-bone steaks

2 tsp/10g crushed garlic

2 tsp/10ml oil

salt and pepper

Garlic Butter

60g/2oz butter

1 tsp/5g crushed garlic

1 tbsp/5g parsley flakes

2 tsp/10ml lemon juice

mix all ingredients together and chill to harden.

Perfect T-Bone Steak

Tip

Many a time this delicious steak has been ruined on the barbecue. The method given here is suitable for any type of barbecue, but improvise a hood if using a flat top barbecue.

Method

1. Combine the ginger, garlic, coriander, olive oil, and lemon juice in a shallow bowl. Place the fillets in the bowl and turn to coat well. Cover and stand 10–15 minutes to marinate.

2. Heat the barbecue to medium-hot and oil the grill bars. Place a sheet of nonstick baking paper over the bars and make a few slashes between the grill bars to allow ventilation. Place the fish on the paper and cook for 3–4 minutes each side according to thickness. Brush with marinade during cooking. Remove to serving platter. Heat any remaining marinade and pour it over the fish.

3. Serve with potato wedges and a salad.

Snapper Fillets with Lemon and Coriander

Ingredients

1 tsp/5g chopped fresh ginger

1 tsp/5g crushed garlic

2 tbsp/15g finely chopped coriander (cilantro)

2 tbsp/30ml olive oil

1½ tbsp/20ml lemon juice

1lb/500g red snapper fillets (4 portions)

Tip

Fish is cooked, if when tested with a fork, it flakes or the sections pull away. Grouper, weakfish, and porgy may also be used.

Method

1. Beat the butter to soften and mix in 1½ tsp of the Cajun seasoning and the chopped chili. Spread a ¼-inch layer of butter along the center of a piece of plastic wrap or nonstick baking paper. Fold the plastic wrap or parchment paper over the butter then roll up as for a burrito. Smooth into a cylinder and twist the ends. Refrigerate until firm.

2. Trim the cutlets if necessary and snip the membrane at the side to stop the meat curling up during cooking.

Flatten the meat lightly with the side of a steak hammer. Mix together 1½ tsp of the Cajun seasoning and olive oil then rub mixture well into both sides of the cutlets. Arrange in a single layer on a pan, cover. and leave for 20 minutes at room temperature, or longer in the refrigerator.

3. Heat the barbecue or electric barbecue grill to high. Place a sheet of nonstick baking paper on the grill bars, making a few slashes between the bars for ventilation. Place cutlets on grill and cook for 3 minutes each side for medium and 4 minutes for well-done. When cooked, transfer to a serving platter and top each cutlet with a pat of Cajun butter. Serve immediately with cooked vegetables.

Cajun Cutlets

Ingredients

For the Cajun butter

½ cup /125g/4oz butter

3 tsp/15g Cajun seasoning

1 small red chili pepper, seeded and chopped

16 small lamb cutlets, with bone

Tip

Serve the cutlets with green beans or salad.

Method

1.Place wings in a large container and smother with the marinade.

Cover and marinade for 30 minutes at room temperature or longer

in the refrigerator.

2. Place half the wings in a microwave-safe dish and microwave

for 10 minutes on high.

Remove and microwave the remainder.

3. Heat the barbecue until hot. Place a wire cake-rack over the grill bars

and place the wings on the rack. Brush with marinade left in the bow.

Turn and brush the wings frequently until they are brown and crisp.

4. Spread sesame seeds on a foil tray and place on the barbecue. Shake

occasionally as they toast. Sprinkle over the browned chicken wings.

Ingredients

4lb/2kg chicken wings, tips trimmed

1 quantity soy and honey marinade (page 9)

3 tbsp sesame seeds,toasted

Quick Sesame Chicken Wings

Tip

Serve as finger food.

Method

1. Mix all patty ingredients together and knead lightly with one hand to distribute the ingredients evenly and create a fine texture. Cover and refrigerate for 20 minutes. With wet hands, form into small flat patties about 1in/2.5cm in diameter. Place on a greased cookie sheet until needed and refrigerate. Combine the ingredients for the Chili Yogurt Sauce.

2. Prepare the batter for pancakes. Sift the flour and salt into a bowl. Combine the basil and garlic with the milk, then beat in the egg. Make a well in the center of the flour and pour in the milk mixture. Stir to form a smooth batter. Cover, and set aside for 20 minutes.

3. Heat the barbecue until hot and oil the grill bars and griddle. Brush the patties with a little oil and place on the grill bars. Grill for 2 minutes each side.

4. While the patties are cooking, grease a griddle and spoon ¼ cup/60ml/2fl oz pancake mixture onto it in dollar-sized rounds. Cook until bubbles appear over the surface then flip with a metal spatula and cook until golden on both sides. Transfer to a clean cloth or paper towel and cover to keep hot.

5. Serve a few small pancakes on each plate with 3 patties, and top with a dollop of Chili Yogurt Sauce.

Chicken Patties served on Basil Pancakes with Chili Yogurt Sauce

Ingredients

For the patties

2 cups/1lb/500g ground chicken

½ tsp salt

¼ tsp pepper

1 tsp/5g crushed garlic

½ tsp fresh chopped chili or chili powder

2 tbsp/15g dry breadcrumbs

¼ cup/60ml/2fl oz water

For the pancakes

1¼ cups/150g/5oz self-rising flour

¼ tsp salt

2 tbsp/30g/1oz chopped basil

1 tsp/5g crushed garlic

¾ cup/180ml/6fl oz milk

1 egg

Chili Yogurt Sauce

1 scant cup/200ml/7oz plain yogurt

2 tsp/10ml sweet chili sauce or to taste

Tip

If self-rising flour is not available, use the same quantity

of all-purpose flour and add ½ tsp/10g baking powder.

Method

1. Cut lamb into 1cm/½in cubes. Place in a bowl and add lemon juice, salt, pepper, oil, and garlic. Cover and marinate at room temperature for 20 minutes. Thread onto skewers.

2. Heat the barbecue and oil the grill bars. Pour the salsa in a foil or metal container and place at side of barbecue to warm through.

3. Cook lamb skewers for 3–4 minutes each side. Halve the pita bread and warm on the barbecue. Remove the lamb from the skewers. Open the pita pocket, fill with lettuce and lamb, and top with heated salsa. Serve immediately.

Lamb and Salsa Pockets

Ingredients

½ leg of lamb (around 3½lb/1½kg)

1 tbsp/½ fl oz/15ml lemon juice

salt and pepper

2 tsp/10ml oil

1 tsp/5g crushed garlic

bamboo skewers, soaked

10oz/300g tomato salsa

6 pita breads

3 cups/12oz/350g shredded lettuce

Method

1. Place coriander, crushed garlic, chopped ginger, oil, and lemon juice in a bowl.

Cut chicken livers in half through the center membrane and carefully stir into the coriander marinade. Cover, and refrigerate for 1 hour or more.

2. Cut each bacon strip into 3 strips around 4in/10cm long.

Wrap a strip of bacon around each liver half and secure with a toothpick.

3. Heat the barbecue until hot. Place an upturned wire cake-rack over the grill bars. Arrange the skewered livers on the rack.

Cook for 8–10 minutes, turning frequently, and brushing with any remaining marinade.

Ingredients

2 tbsp/30g finely chopped coriander

1 tsp/5g crushed garlic

1 tsp/5g chopped fresh ginger

2 tsp/10ml olive oil

1 tbsp/15ml lemon juice

1 cup/8oz/250g chicken livers

6 thin slices lean bacon

toothpicks

Skewered Chicken Livers with Bacon

Tip

Serve as finger food.

Cook on any flat-top barbecue

or electric barbecue grill.

barbecue

Method

1. Place sausages in a large saucepan and cover with cold water. Heat slowly until simmering point is reached, then simmer for 5 minutes. Drain well. If not required immediately refrigerate until needed.

2. Heat the barbecue until hot and grease grill bars with oil. Pour the honey and chili marinade into a heatproof bowl and place at the side of the barbecue. Arrange sausages from left to right on the grill bars or griddle and brush with the marinade. Turn and brush with marinade after one minute and continue turning and basting for 10 minutes, or until sausages are well glazed and cooked through. Give a final brushing with marinade as they are removed to a serving platter.

3. To cook the onions, oil the hot plate and place the onion slices on it. Toss at intervals, drizzling with a little oil as they cook. Serve the honey-glazed sausages with the onions and accompany with salad and garlic bread.

Ingredients

4lb/2kg/ pork or beef boiling sausages

2lb/1kg onions, thinly sliced

Honey & chili marinade (page 8)

Quick Sausage Sizzle

Note:

This method is suitable for cooking a large number of sausages.

Thick pork or beef boiling sausages, such as frankfurters, wieners, or

kielbasa are suitable. They should be poached in water for

at least 10 minutes, before being barbecued.

This prevents thick sausages from splitting, ensures they are cooked right through,

and reduces barbecuing time. The amount

of sausages needed depends on the number of diners, allow two per diner.

Method

1. Mix all the Kofta ingredients together and combine well by hand to distribute ingredients evenly and make the texture finer.

2. With wet hands, shape tablespoons of mixture into 2in/5cm long cylinder shapes and flatten   slightly.

3. Heat the barbecue to medium-high and oil the grill bars or griddle. Place the Koftas on the grill and cook for 15 minutes, turning frequently. Brush with a little oil as they cook.

4. Combine the yogurt, tandoori paste, and lemon juice. Arrange salad greens on a serving platter.

5. When Koftas are cooked, transfer to the platter. Drizzle with yogurt sauce or serve the sauce in a bowl on the platter.

Ingredients

For the Kofta

2 cups/1lb/500g ground chicken

½ cup/60g/2oz dry breadcrumbs

1 medium onion, minced

1 tbsp/½ oz/15g chopped parsley

½ tsp salt

¼ tsp pepper

Tandoori paste (page 8)

Tandoori Chicken Kofta

barbecue

Method

1. To make marinade, combine sun-dried tomato pesto,chopped basil, lemon juice, and olive oil.

2. Carefully remove the silvery white membrane from the top of the fillets with a sharp, pointed knife. Place fillets in a suitable container and cover both sides with half of the marinade, reserving the remainder. Cover and marinate for 30 minutes at room temperature, or longer in the refrigerator.

3. Cook as follows:

Charcoal Kettle or Hooded Gas Barbecue: Prepare barbecue for indirect cooking. Place the fillets on oiled grill bars over the drip-pan. Cook, covered with lid for around 40 minutes.

Brush twice with some of the remaining marinade mixture. When the fillets are almost cooked, make the hot cakes. Remove them from the dish, and brush with oil. Place over direct heat and cook for 4 minutes on each side until golden.

Flat-top and Electric Barbecue Grills: Heat until hot. Place a wire cake-rack to stand 1in/2.5cm above grill bars. Place fillets on cake-rack and cook for approximately 20 minutes each side. Brush with marinade after turning. Serve with the hot cakes.

Spicy Pork Fillets with Hot Cakes

Ingredients

4 pork fillets 10oz/300g each)

5½oz/165g jar sun-dried tomato pesto

1 tbsp/15g chopped basil

2 tbsp/1 fl oz/30ml lemon juice

1 tbsp/15ml olive oil

1 quantity hot cakes (see page 64)

To serve:

Slice the fillets into 1in/2.5cm thick diagonal slices. Place over the hot cakes slices. Warm the rest of the tomato mixture and pour it over the fish. Serve with mixed leaf salad.

barbecue

Method

1. Gut and descale the fish and rinse well. Pat dry with paper towels.

2. Combine the bell pepper, basil, lemon juice, and oil. Spoon some of this mixture into the cavity and spread the remainder over the fish.

3. Lay the fish on a large sheet of oiled aluminum foil.

4. Charcoal Broiler and Hooded Gas Barbecue: Roll up the edges of foil around the fish, leaving the top of the fish exposed. Place the fish on the grill bars, and cook over indirect heat. Cover with lid or hood and cook for 35–40 minutes or until fish flakes when tested with a fork.

Flat Top Charcoal or Gas Barbecue: Cover the fish completely with foil.

Place on a wire rack over the grill bars, raised so that the fish is 4 in/10cm above the heat source. Cook for 10–12 minutes each side. Turn carefully, using a large spatula or place fish in a hinged fish barbecuing-rack and turn when required.

Electric Barbecue Grill: Prepare as for kettle barbecue, and place on raised wire rack place over grill bars. Set barbecue to medium high. Cover with hood and cook 25–35 minutes.

To make the Pickle Mayonnaise, mix the mayonnaise and pickle relish or chopped pickles together.

Serve the fish while hot with pickle mayonnaise and accompany with potato wedges or home fries, and salad.

Ingredients

1 whole red snapper (3lb/1.5kg)

3 tbsp/45g chopped red bell peppers

2 tsp/10g chopped fresh basil

2 tbsp/1 fl oz/60ml lemon juice

1 tbsp/30ml olive oil

Barbecued Whole Red Snapper with Pickle Mayonnaise Relish

For the pickle mayonnaise

1 cup/8fl oz/250ml mayonnaise

⅓ cup/3fl oz/80ml pickle relish or finely chopped pickles

Method

1.Place spare ribs on a large sheet of heavy-duty aluminum foil and cover both sides generously with marinade. Wrap, burrito-style, into a double-folded package, making sure all joins are well-sealed to prevent leakage. Leave to marinate for at least 30 minutes before cooking. Place in refrigerator if not to be cooked immediately.

2. Prepare the barbecue for direct-heat cooking. Place a wire cake-rack on the grill bars to stand 1in/2.5cm above the bars. Place ribs in the foil package on the rack and cook 10 minutes each side.

3. Remove to a plate, open package, remove ribs, and discard foil. Return the ribs to rack and continue cooking, brushing with fresh sauce or marinade and turning frequently until ribs are well browned and crisp (about 10 minutes). Total cooking time is approximately 30–35 minutes.

Glazed Pork Spare Ribs

Ingredients

2½lb/1kg/ pork spare ribs or short ribs

soy and honey marinade (page 9)

Note:

Ribs may be cooked by indirect heat in a hooded barbecue, in which case there is no need to wrap them in foil. Place over indirect heat after marinating. Brush and turn frequently with lid down for 1 hour or more. Cooking in aluminum foil over direct heat cuts cooking time in half.

Tip

The ribs can be cooked on any type of bar-

becue using direct heat.

Method

1. Place pork cubes in a nonmetallic container and coat thoroughly with the sauce. Cover and marinate for 30 minutes at room temperature, or longer in refrigerator.

2. Thread pork cubes onto skewers alternately with the pineapple, bell pepper, and onion pieces. Brush with marinade and cook according to barbecue type,
as follows:

Charcoal-fueled kettle barbecues and hooded gas barbecues: Prepare barbecue for indirect heat. Place skewers on oiled grill bars and brush well with marinade. Cook with lid or hood down for 25–30 minutes, turn once or twice, and brush with marinade.

Flat-top and electric barbecue grill: Place a wire cake-rack so that it sits 1in/2.5cm above the grill bars. Heat barbecue until hot. Place the kabobs on grill and brush with marinade.

Turn after 5 minutes and brush again. Continue to cook for a total time of around 25 minutes.

Ingredients

2lb/1kg lean, boneless pork cut into 1in/2.5cm cubes

soy and honey marinade (page 9)

½ fresh pineapple cut into 1in/2.5cm cubes

2 red bell peppers, cut into 1in/2cm/ squares

1 small onion, quartered

8 bamboo skewers, soaked,

or 8 metal skewers

Hawaiian Pork Kabobs

Serve these kabobs with plenty of green salad and hand unsweetened shredded coconut with it for guests to sprinkle on the kabobs.

Method

1. Cook sausages as directed on page 35. When cooked, slit each sausage almost through. Open out the slit and sprinkle it with some of the crushed corn tortilla chips. Spoon in a generous amount of salsa and top with grated cheese. Return to the barbecue grill, carefully arranged so that the filling does not spill out.

2. Cover the barbecue with lid or hood and cook until cheese melts, about 1 minute. If using a flat-top or electric barbecue grill, improvise a cover by using a large saucepan lid or upturned roasting pan to enclose heat so cheese can melt.

Mexican Weenies

Ingredients

2lb/1kg frankfurters or wieners (page 35)

2 small packages (2oz/50g) corn tortilla chips,

lightly crushed

1 cup/8oz/250ml tomato salsa

⅔ cup/3½oz/100g/ grated sharp cheddar

cheese

Method

1. Split chicken in half, cutting through the breast bone and backbone with a cleaver or large, sharp knife. Place chicken, cut side downward, on a board and press down on the breast with the heel of your hand to flatten it. Place in a non-metallic, wide bowl. Prepare the tandoori paste and rub it all over the chicken. Cover and marinate for several hours in the refrigerator.

2. Heat the barbecue and place chicken on the grill bars over a drip tray. Cover the barbecue with a lid and cook, skin side upward, for 40–45 minutes, basting occasionally with any left-over tandoori paste.

3. Serve on a bed of chicory or escarole. Accompany with tomato-and-chili relish, or other relish of your choice.

Ingredients

2 x medium roasting chickens (1½kg/3 lb)

1 quantity tandoori paste (page 89)

¼ cup/2 fl oz/60ml lemon juice

1 head chicory or escarole for serving

tomato and chili relish for serving

Tandoori Chicken Halves

barbecue

Tip

For best results cook in a kettle

barbecue, over charcoal.

Method

1. **Truss** the roast with kitchen string to give it a compact shape. The roast has a half-moon shape and the outer edges will dry if the roast is not tied.

2. **In a glass** bowl, combine the other ingredients. Add the lamb and turn to coat on all sides. Marinate for 1 hour at room temperature, or longer in the refrigerator.

3. **Prepare** barbecue for indirect heat. Place lamb over drip pan in the center of barbecue to use indirect heat, cover with lid or hood, and cook for 35–40 minutes. There is no need to turn it. Or place lamb in foil tray in same position on rack so cooking juices will be retained. Brush with marinade as it cooks, turn the meat once or twice during cooking.

Barbecued Noodles:

1. **Rinse** the noodles in hot water and separate. Drain thoroughly.

Mix coriander, feta cheese, garlic, and chili to a paste.

2. **Heat** the barbecue griddle or use a metal baking pan on the griddle.

Oil the griddle or pan, add the noodles, and toss while adding the coriander paste. Mix well and heat through.

3. **Arrange** on a serving platter.

4. **Slice** lamb and arrange the slices over noodles. Sprinkle with any remaining pan juices.

Ingredients

1 small boneless lamb roast (about 2½lb/1kg)

2 tbsp/30g chopped fresh coriander (cilantro)

1 tsp/5g crushed garlic

1 tbsp/5ml lemon juice

salt and pepper

1 tbsp/15ml oil

Mini Lamb Roast with Barbecued Noodles

Barbecued Noodles

1 tbsp/15g chopped fresh coriander(cilantro)

100g/3oz feta cheese, crumbled

1 tsp/5g crushed garlic

½ tsp/2.5g chopped red chili pepper (optional)

500g/1lb Hokkien (thick wheat) noodles

barbecue

Method

1. **Trim** some of the fat from the racks, leaving a thin layer on them. Rub all over with a little crushed garlic. Combine the rest of the ingredients and pack them over each rack. Place the lamb on a cookie sheet, cover with plastic wrap. and refrigerate for at least 1 hour.

2. **Cook** as directed below and serve with Basil Tomatoes and Bruschetta.

Kettle or Hooded Gas Barbecue: Prepare barbecue for indirect heat. Place racks of lamb, in pairs, back-to-back for support, on the oiled grill bars, over the drip pan, in an upright position. Cover with lid or hood and cook for 35–45 minutes. Remove from barbecue, cover with foil, and leave to rest 5 minutes before serving.

Basil Tomatoes: Cross-cut cherry tomatoes, sprinkle with a little chopped basil, and place in foil tray. Cover with foil, and cook 10 minutes on side of barbecue.

Basil Bruschetta: Slice the bread into 1½ cm/½in slices. Mix the ricotta with the chopped basil. Spread onto the bread slices. Place the slices on the barbecue, cheese side up, and toast for 2 minutes. **Place** a piece of nonstick baking paper on grill bars and turn cheese side down on the paper. Cook 1–2 minutes until cheese has colored slightly and the grill-bar markings are defined.

Tip

For best results, prepare the lamb the night before.

Allow 2–3 cutlets per serving. Not suitable

for flat-top barbecue.

Pesto Crusted Racks of Lamb with Tomatoes and Basil Bruschetta

Ingredients

4 to 6 racks lamb (4lb/1½kg), 3 to 4 cutlets on each

3 cups/180g/6oz soft, white breadcrumbs

¼ cup/30g/1oz pine nuts

3 tbsp/45g fresh chopped basil

1 tsp/5g crushed garlic

2 tbsp/30g grated Romano or Parmesan cheese

1 tbsp/15ml lemon juice

1 small egg (55g/2oz), lightly beaten

Basil Tomatoes

cherry tomatoes

2 tbsp/30g fresh basil, chopped

Basil Bruschetta

1 loaf whole-wheat or rye bread

1 scant cup/200g/7oz ricotta cheese

2 tbsp/30g fresh basil, chopped

Method

1. **Rinse** chicken inside and out, making sure any remaining giblets in the cavity are removed. Rinse cavity well, stand upright to drain, and pat dry with paper towels. Brush the chicken inside and out with barbecue sauce. Place the chicken in the center of a large foil baking dish and surround with prepared potatoes and onions. Combine the lemon juice, garlic, salt, pepper, water, and oil and pour the mixture over the potatoes.

2. **Cook** as follows:

Kettle or Hooded Gas Barbecue: Place the tray containing chicken and potatoes on the grill bars over indirect heat. Cover with lid and cook for 50 minutes.

Turn potatoes and brush chicken with barbecue sauce. Continue to brush chicken every 10 minutes during total cooking time of 1¼ to 1½ hours. The chicken is done if juices run clear when pricked with a skewer. Leave to stand 10 minutes before carving. Remove potatoes from tray when cooked. The chicken and potatoes may be browned over direct heat if liked.

Electric Barbecue Grill with Hood: Place dish containing chicken and potatoes on a wire cake-rack standing 1in/2.5cm above the grill bars. Cook on medium-high heat, as directed above.

Ingredients

1 large roasting chicken (4lb/1½kg

1 cup/250 ml/8oz barbecue sauce

1kg/2lb potatoes, washed, peeled, and cut into pieces

1 tbsp/15ml lemon juice

Barbecued Chicken and Potatoes

1 tsp/5g crushed garlic

5 small pickling onions

¼ cup/60ml/2fl oz water

2 tbsp/30ml oil

Method

1. Wash the lamb and pat dry. Make about 8 incisions on each side of the meat with the point of a small knife. Place the meat in a suitable non-corrosive pan, rub all over with salt and pepper and pour the lemon juice over it, allowing the juice to enter the incisions. Stand 30 minutes. Push a ½ tsp minced garlic into each incision, followed by a cheese cube. Rub all over with tomato pesto. Wrap the lamb in the 2 sheets of oiled parchment or nonstick baking paper, and then wrap with the brown paper to make package. Tie securely with kitchen string.

2. Prepare Kettle or Gas Hooded Barbecue for indirect heat on medium-high. Place the lamb package onto the oiled grill bars over a drip tray and cook in indirect heat for 2 hours. Turn the lamb after 1 hour. When cooked, remove from barbecue and rest for 20 minutes before removing from paper. Take care, when opening package, that any juices are collected in a bowl. Reheat juices and serve with the carved meat.

3. Serve with a mild mustard, a green salad, and garlic bread.

Ingredients

5lb/2kg leg of lamb

2 tsp/10g salt

1 tsp/5g freshly ground black pepper

½ cup/125ml/4fl oz lemon juice

2 tbsp/30g minced garlic

Romano or Parmesan cheese, cut into 8 x 0.5 cm/¼ in cubes

165g/5½oz jar sun-dried tomato pesto

Barbecued Leg of Lamb in Paper

2 sheets parchment or nonstick baking paper,
oiled

1 sheet brown paper, oiled on both sides

Method

1. It is best to order a loin of pork with the rind on from your butcher, a couple of days in advance.

2. Score the rind in a diamond pattern using a sharp, pointed knife. Combine the stuffing ingredients and spread the mixture over the underside of the roast, leaving a border. Roll up the meat tightly, so that the rind covers the outside, and fasted with skewers. Truss the meat with kitchen string at 1in/2.5cm intervals, then remove the skewers.

3. Rub the sun-dried tomato pesto over the surface of the rolled roast.

Cook as follows:

Kettle and Hooded Gas Barbecue: Prepare barbecue for indirect, normal or medium heat. Place the meat over the drip pan, cover with the lid or hood, and cook for 50 minutes. Start basting with the marinade every 10 minutes for a further 45–55 minutes. The total cooking time should be approximately 1¼ to 1¾ hours. If using a meat thermometer, the inside temperature should reach (167°F–171°F (75°C–77°C).

Electric Barbecue Grill with Hood: Set temperature to medium high.

Place roast in a foil pan and stand on a wire cake-rack raised 1 in/2.5cm above the grill bars. Cover with hood and cook as above.

4. When cooked, wrap the meat in foil and let stand 15 minutes before carving. Slice the roast and serve garnished with small stuffed apples (page 90) and cooked vegetables of your choice.

Ingredients

1½ kg/3lb boned loin of park with rind

1 tbsp/15g sun-dried tomato pesto

1 tbsp/15ml honey & chili marinade (page 8)

Loin of Pork with Sun-dried Tomato and Apple Stuffing

Sun-dried Tomato and Apple Stuffing

1 cup/60g/2oz soft white, breadcrumbs

2 tbsp/30g sun-dried tomato pesto

1 red apple, finely diced

1 tbsp honey & chili marinade (page 8)

salt and pepper

barbecue

Method

Cut into the thick part of the turkey breast, holding the knife in an angle of 45° and cut through the breast almost completely. Open the meat out and beat it with a steak hammer until it is of uniform thickness. **Rub** the meat with salt and pepper. **Mix** all ingredients for the stuffing and stuff it in the length of the cut down the center of the meat. Roll the meat around a skewer into a 2.5cm/1in thick roll with kitchen twine, and remove the skewer. **Grill** the meat as follows:

Charcoal or gas barbecue with lid:

Set the barbecue to the indirect grilling method and place it at medium height. Grease the grill rack and place the turkey roll over the drip pan. Close the lid of the barbecue and grill the meat for 20 minutes, after which baste the meat with the marinade every 15 minutes, until done. The turkey is done when it is pricked with a skewer and the juices runs clear. The total cooking time should be around 1 hour.

Electric barbecue grill with lid:

Heat the barbecue to grill temperature. Put the turkey roll in an aluminum foil pan and set this on grill bars above the grill. Close the lid of the barbecue and follow the instructions as indicated above. **Remove** the turkey from the barbecue and let it rest for 10 minutes until it partially opens. Serve the roll with glazed sweet potatoes and potato puffs. Mix the juices with a little of the marinade and serve this as sauce with the meat.

Ingredients

1 turkey breast, around 2½lb/1.3kg

salt, pepper

½ cup/120ml/4oz red wine & garlic marinade (page 9)

Stuffed Rolled Turkey Breast

Stuffing

1 medium onion, minced

2 cups/120g/4oz fresh breadcrumbs

150g/5oz lean, cooked ham, chopped

2 tbsp minced parsley

2 tbsp/30ml red wine

Method

1. **Grease** an aluminum foil baking tray, and arrange with the sweet potato slices on it. Add the water. Brush the top of the sweet potato with the red wine marinade. Cover the tray with foil, place on the griddle, and cook 10 minutes. Remove the foil, turn slices over, and brush with more marinade.

Continue to cook, uncovered, until tender and well glazed.

Note: Ordinary white potatoes may also be used.

Glazed Sweet Potatoes

Ingredients

2lb/1kg sweet potatoes, peeled and sliced

1 tbsp/15ml water

1 cup/240ml/8fl oz red wine & garlic marinade (page 9)

Method

1. **Sift** the flour and salt together into a bowl.

2. **Beat** together the milk, egg, garlic, and parsley flakes, pour into the flour all at once. Stir lightly just until incorporated. Do not overmix.

3. **Grease** a heated griddle on the barbecue. The best way to do this is to grip a wad of kitchen paper with tongs, dip the top of the wad in oil and rub it over the griddle.

4. **Drop** one tablespoon of the mixture from the tip of a spoon onto the griddle. When bubbles appear on the surface, turn with metal spatula, to cook other side.

5. **As the hot** cakes cook, lift them into a cloth-lined tray or basket. Cover and serve warm, topped with sour cream or cream cheese and a teaspoon of relish.

Garlic Hot Cakes with Sour Cream and Relish

Ingredients

1 cup/125g/4oz self-rising flour

pinch salt

½ cup/120ml/4fl oz milk

1 egg

1 tsp crushed garlic

1 tsp/5g parsley flakes

1¼ cups/300g/10fl oz sour cream

260g/9oz jar mixed vegetable relish

Method

1. **Toss** potatoes with oil and salt to coat. Wrap each potato in a piece of foil.

Place on the barbecue for 20–25 minutes, turning every 5 minutes.

Split open, and serve with sour cream mixed with the Dijon-style mustard.

Tip

Cook over indirect heat in a covered barbecue.

Jacket Potatoes

Ingredients

1kg/2¼lb baking potatoes, washed

½ cup/120ml/4fl oz olive oil

3 tsp/15g salt

1 cup/240g/8oz sour cream

2 tbsp/30ml Dijon-style mustard

Method

1. **Rinse noodles** in hot water and separate. Drain thoroughly. Combine the prepared vegetables. Place the teriyaki marinade in a small saucepan to heat.

2. **Heat** the barbecue griddle to medium-high and oil well. Pile on noodles, toss lightly, and add vegetables. Lift and toss with tongs to mix through, then begin splashing the heated marinade over them. When well mixed and heated through, remove to a hot serving platter. Serve immediately.

Method

1. **Peel** and halve the potatoes, then cut each half into 4–6 wedges.

Rinse well and drain, then place in a large bowl. Mix garlic, basil pesto, olive oil, and water together. Pour this over the potatoes and toss to coat well. Place in a large aluminum foil dish, in a single layer if possible, and pour over any basil oil mixture remaining in the bowl.

2. **Cook** over indirect heat in a covered barbecue for 40 minutes, turning after 20 minutes.

For flat top barbecues, cover with a sheet of foil and place in the foil tray on the griddle. Cook 20 minutes, then turn and cook 20 minutes more until tender.

3. **When** cooked, remove to a plate and sprinkle with Parmesan cheese.

Noodle and Vegetable Medley & **Pesto** Potato Wedges

Ingredients	Ingredients
450g/15oz Hokkein (thick, wheat) noodles	4 medium-sized potatoes
1 large carrot, coarsely grated	1 tsp/5g minced garlic
2 zucchini, grated	2 tbsp/30ml basil pesto
6 shallots, chopped into 2.5cm/1in pieces	1 tbsp/15ml water
1 cup/250ml/8fl oz teriyaki marinade (page 8)	1/2 cup/60g/2oz grated Parmesan cheese

Pesto Tomatoes

1. **Slice across** the top of tomato, leaving the lid attached. Mix the basil and grated cheese together, lift tomato lid, and spread the mixture onto the cut surface. Replace the lid and sprinkle a little of the mixture on top. Stand in a foil tray and place the tray on the barbecue. Cover with a lid or hood and cook for 15 minutes. If a flattop barbecue is used, cover the tomatoes with foil.

Quick Ratatouille

1. **Prepare** the vegetables. Oil a large foil tray and spread it with some of the salsa. Layer in the vegetables, spreading salsa between each layer. Cover with more salsa. Place over indirect heat in a covered barbecue and cook for 30 minutes. For a flattop barbecue, cover the tray with foil, stand on a cake-rake placed over the grill bars and cook for 30 minutes.

Pesto Tomatoes &
Quick Ratatouille

Ingredients

2 medium-sized eggplant,

cut into 1cm/½in slices

4 zucchini, cut into 1cm/½in slices

1 large onion, cut in half and sliced

1 green bell pepper, seeded, and sliced

300g/10oz jar tomato salsa

1 tsp/5g crushed garlic

Ingredients

12 small even sized tomatoes

2 tbsp/30ml basil pesto

2 tbsp/30g grated Romano or Parmesan cheese

Method

1. **Place** chicken breast pieces in a non-metallic dish and stir in enough marinade to coat well. Cover and stand to marinate 30 minutes, or longer in refrigerator.

Cook rice in boiling, salted water until tender, about 15 minutes. Drain well.

Boil beans until tender but still crisp, and drain them. Mix the rice, beans, and half the roasted peanuts together. Keep hot.

2. **Place** a sheet of baking paper on top of the hot grill bars and place the breast pieces on the paper. Cook for 2 minutes on each side on high heat, brushing with marinade during cooking.

Heat the extra marinade, about ½ cup/125ml/4oz, at the side of the barbecue.

3. Pile rice into center of the heated plates. Arrange 2 or 3 pieces of chicken breast over the rice, top with the heated satay marinade, and sprinkle with the remaining roasted peanuts.

Ingredients

500g/1lb chicken breasts, cut into serving pieces

1 cup/250ml/8fl oz satay marinade (page 8)

1½ cups/270g/9oz uncooked rice

1 scant cup/200g/7oz green beans, topped, tailed, and halved

50g/2oz roasted unsalted peanuts

Chicken Gado

Method

1. **Mix** the ginger, chili, oil, lime juice, and zest together. Pour half into a shallow serving platter. Place the salmon cutlets in the dish and pour over the remaining marinade. Allow to stand for 20 minutes before cooking.

2. **Heat** the flat-top or electric barbecue grill to medium-high and oil the grill bars. Cook the salmon cutlets for 4–5 minutes on each side, brushing with the marinade as they cook. **While** cooking, place the blanched snowpeas in foil and reheat on the barbecue. Slice the potatoes into ½in/1cm slices. Brush with oil and cook on the griddle or grill bars a few minutes on each side.

Serve immediately.

Ginger Salmon Steaks with Snowpeas and Potatoes

Ingredients

2 tsp/10g chopped ginger

½ tsp/2.5g chopped chili pepper

2 tbsp/30ml oil   4 salmon cutlets

1 tbsp/15ml lime juice   3 medium sized potatoes, parboiled in their jackets

2 tsp/10g grated lime zest   2 scant cups/200g/7oz snowpeas, blanched

Method

1. **Trim** the lamb fillets, removing the fine silver membrane. Place in a dish and add garlic, lemon juice, oil, salt, and pepper. Cover and stand 30 minutes.

Cook the rice in the boiling, salted water, about 15 minutes, or until tender. Drain well and keep hot. Heat a small saucepan, add pine nuts, and shake over heat until they color. Add the salsa and currants and heat through.

2. Heat the barbecue grill plate and oil lightly. Set at medium-high. Place lamb on grill and cook 6-8 minutes, turning frequently. Cook longer for well done. Allow to rest 5 minutes before slicing in 1cm/1/2 in slices.

3. To Serve: Using a cup or mould, form a mound of rice on the plate. Pour salsa over the rice and arrange lamb slices at base of rice mould.

Ingredients

2 lamb fillets (about 750g/11/2 lb)

1/2 tsp crushed garlic

1 tbsp lemon juice

2 tsp olive oil

salt & pepper

Lamb Fillets with Salsa Pilaf

barbecue

Salsa Pilaf

1½ cups/240g/8oz uncooked rice

6 cups/1½ l/3½ pints boiling water

60g/2oz pine nuts, toasted

1¼ cups/300ml/10 fl oz tomato salsa

2 tbsp/30g currants

Method

1. Cream the butter until soft and mix in the coriander and parmesan.
Pile into butter pot and set aside.

2. Heat barbecue grill until hot and brush with oil. Brush fish steaks with oil,
place on grill bars and cook 3-4 minutes each side according to thickness.
Brush or spray vegetables with oil and place on grill, cook a few minutes on each
side. Remove fish steaks and vegetables to heated plates. Top swordfish steak with
a generous piece of coriander butter mixture and serve immediately.

Coriander Swordfish Steaks

Ingredients

125g/4oz unsalted butter	4 swordfish steaks
2 tbsp finely chopped	1 tbsp olive oil
coriander	4 zucchini, cut into long slices
1 tbsp grated parmesan cheese	1 red bell pepper, quartered

Method

1. Slice the eggplant lengthwise into ½in/1cm slices.

2. Heat the barbecue grill and griddle to medium-high and oil well.
Brush eggplant with oil and place on barbecue. Cook about 4 minutes on
each side until pinkish- brown. Place the salsa in a small container at the side
of barbecue. As eggplants cook, spread one slice with salsa topped with second
slice of eggplant. Spread again with salsa and place a cheese slice on top.
Cover with lid or hood and cook until cheese starts to melt and encases the stack.
If cooking on a flattop, use a suitable saucepan lid or baking dish to cover.

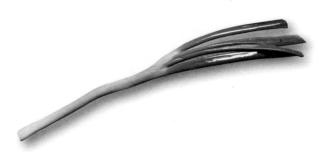

Eggplant Stacks

Ingredients

2 or 3 large eggplant

½ cup/120ml/4fl oz olive oil

1¼ cups/300g/10oz tomato salsa

6 – 8 slices Cheddar or Mozzarella cheese

Method

1. Place the steaks in a shallow dish. Combine the garlic, chili, oil, salt, and pepper and pour this over the steaks. Cover and stand 30 minutes.

2. Heat the barbecue grill to high and oil the bars. Sear the meat for 2 minutes on each side then reduce the heat slightly or move steaks to cooler part of barbecue and cook 8 minutes on each side. Brush with marinade during cooking. Leave to rest for 5 minutes before slicing.

3. Slice the meat thinly and arrange on it on a platter covered with salad greens. Mix dressing ingredients together and pour over the beef.

Serve immediately with Barbecue Toast (page 84).

Ingredients

2 boneless beef tenderloins, 2½cm/1 in thick

½ tsp/2.5g crushed garlic

1 tsp/5g chopped chili

2 tsp/10ml oil

salt and pepper

mixed salad greens for serving

Hot Herbed Beef Salad

Herb Dressing

2 tsp basil pesto

1 tsp chopped chili

1 tbsp chopped parsley

1/2 cup/30g/1oz chopped shallots

1/2 cup/120ml/4fl oz olive oil

1/4 cup/60ml/2fl oz vinegar

barbecue

Method

1. **Remove** the white connective tissue from the pork, then rub all over with

coriander paste.

Cover and stand 30 minutes at room temperature. Meanwhile, prepare the mash.

Boil the potatoes and sweet potato until tender. Drain and return to the hot

saucepan. Mash with a potato masher, add butter, milk, garlic and coriander.

Whip well until smooth. Cover and keep hot.

2. **Heat** the barbecue grill bars to medium-high. Place pork fillet on grill and turn

to sear on all sides. Lower heat and continue to cook for about 12/15 minutes

until done to taste. Rest the fillet for 5 minutes wrapped in foil then cut into thick

diagonal slices. Mound garlic and coriander mash on a plate and arrange slices

of pork. Serve immediately.

Ingredients

1 pork fillet (about 500g/1lb)

1 tbsp/15g chopped coriander

Coriander Creamed Potatoes

3 cups/400g/13oz potatoes peeled and sliced

1 cup/200g/7oz sweet potato, peeled and sliced

boiling, salted water

1 tsp/5g butter

Pork Fillets with Garlic and Coriander Creamed Potatoes

½ cup/120ml/4fl oz milk

1½ tsp/7.5g crushed garlic

2 tbsp/30g chopped coriander

Method

1. **Flatten** chicken breasts lightly with steak hammer to even thickness.

Mix Thai seasoning with the oil together and rub well into the chicken.

Cover and leave to stand 20 minutes before cooking.

2. **Heat** the barbecue to medium-high and oil griddle and grill bars. Place chicken on grill and cook 4 minutes on each side. **Place** vegetables on the griddle, sprinkle with a little oil, and cook for 5-8 minutes, stirring to cook through.

Pile lettuce onto individual plates and place barbecued vegetables in the center.

Cut the chicken into thin diagonal slices and arrange over and around vegetables.

3. **Mix** dressing ingredients together. Pour them over the chicken and warm salad.

Serve with crusty bread.

Tip

The vegetables can also be stir-fried in a wok.

Ingredients

3 chicken breasts

2 tsp/10ml Thai seasoning

1 tsp/5ml oil

1 red bell pepper, seeded and cut into strips

1 green bell pepper, seeded and cut into strips

1 eggplant, cut into slices

1 purple onion, cut into rings

½ romaine lettuce, shredded

Warm Thai Chicken Salad

Dressing

½ cup/120ml/4fl oz olive oil

¼ cup/60ml/2fl oz wine vinegar

1 tsp/5ml Thai seasoning

Method

1. Rub the chicken fillets with the tandoori paste. Sprinkle with a little extra paste, then cover and marinate for at least 30 minutes before cooking.

2. Mix the yogurt, diced cucumber, and remaining tandoori paste together. Cover and refrigerate until ready to serve.

3. Heat the barbecue to medium-high and oil the grill bars. Place a piece of nonstick baking paper over the grill bars. Arrange the chicken on it and cook for 3-4 minutes each side. Place the zucchini slices onto well-oiled grill bars and cook both sides until tender but still crisp.

4. Slice the chicken on the diagonal. Place the zucchini slices on the plate, arrange the chicken slices over them and coat with yogurt sauce.

Serve with hot, boiled rice and a tablespoon of tomato chili relish.

Yogurt Sauce

2 cups/500ml/16 fl oz plain yogurt

2 small cucumbers, diced

2 tbsp/30g tandoori paste

3–4 zucchini, sliced

2 cups boiled rice for serving

1 cup/250g/8oz tomato & chili relish

Ingredients

4 chicken breast fillets

2 tbsp/30g tandoori paste (page 8)

Tandoori Chicken with Yogurt Sauce

barbecue

Tip

Serve with boiled rice, tomatoes, and pickled chili peppers.

Peppered Pineapple

1. Combine the chopped chili, brown sugar, and melted butter.

2. Peel the pineapple, cut it into rings, and remove the core. Place on heated and oiled grill bars. Cook 1 minute on each side then brush with chili mixture and cook 2 minutes each side. Serve with barbecued sausages and meats.

Stuffed apples

1. Core the apples cutting out more apple flesh to widen the hole. Chop the flesh finely and add to the bread crumbs. Add remaining ingredients and mix well. Pack the stuffing into the apples. Place apples in a foil tray and brush with honey & chili marinade.

2. Place on barbecue, using indirect heat, or elevate on wire rack over direct heat. Cover with lid or hood and cook for 30 minutes. Serve as an accompaniment to roast pork or roast turkey.

Stuffed Mushrooms

1. Trim the mushroom stalks. Combine the stuffing ingredients and spoon generously into each mushroom. Sprinkle with a little extra Parmesan cheese.

2. Place on barbecue, cover, and grill for 5 minutes, or until tender.

Stuffed Mushrooms & Apples
Peppered Pineapple

Stuffed Mushrooms

12 medium mushrooms

½ red bell pepper, finely chopped

1 cup/60g/2oz fresh bread crumbs

1 tsp/5g crushed garlic

1 tbsp/15g minced parsley

1 scallion (green onion), minced

½ cup/60 g/2oz grated Parmesan cheese

2 tbsp/30ml melted butter

Peppered Pineapple

1 small ripe, pineapple

1 tsp/5g chopped chili

1 tbsp/15g soft brown sugar

1 tbsp/15ml melted butter

Stuffed apples

6 small, red crisp apples

2½ cups/150g/5oz fresh white bread crumbs

1 small onion, minced

salt and pepper

2 tbsp honey & chili marinade (page 9)

1 tbsp yellow raisins

Method

1. **Peel** the melons, remove seeds, and cut into large cubes. Pour the marinade into an aluminum foil pan and place on the heated griddle. When it begins to bubble, add the melon cubes. **Cook** a few minutes, turn the cubes, and baste with the marinade to glaze. Remove and serve with barbecued meats and chicken.

Melon Medley Salsa

Ingredients

½ Crenshaw melon

½ honeydew melon

½ cup/120g/4oz red wine and garlic marinade (page 9)

Method

1. Mix one part butter or margarine with one part flavoring to taste. Lightly spread both sides of sliced bread or rolls with flavored butter of your choice. Place on heated hot plate and cook until golden on both sides.

Ingredients

Breads

Focaccia

Whole-wheat bread

English muffins

Kaiser rolls

Sourdough bread, sliced

Barbecue Toast

Butters

butter or margarine

tandoori paste (page 8)

Thai seasoning

pesto

Index